FROZEN

Disney
FROZEN

FROZEN

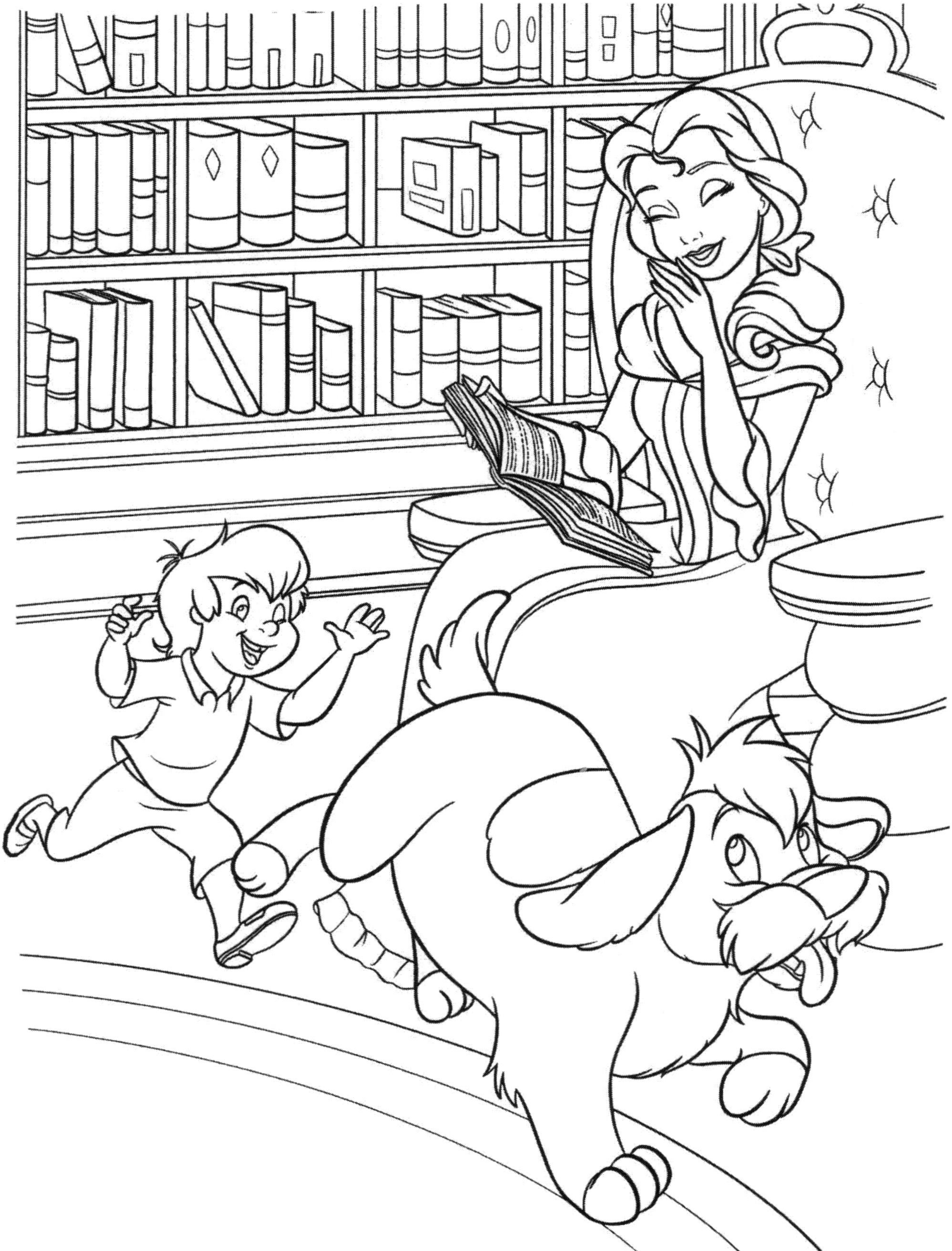

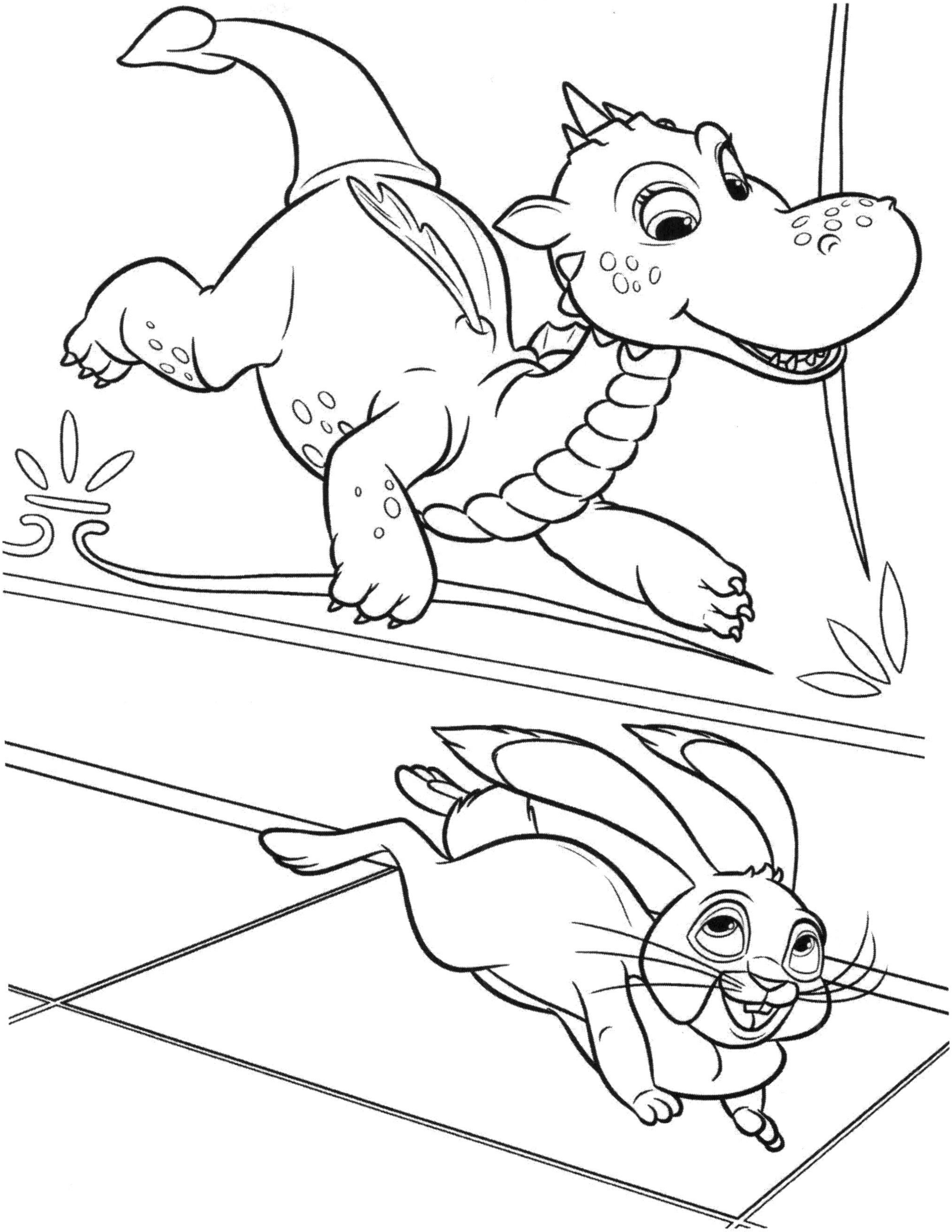

Pokémon
Coloring Book
1

TRANS FORMERS
COLORING BOOK

Pokémon
Coloring Book
2

Disney PIXAR
FINDING DORY
COLORING BOOK

SUPER MARIO
50 ILLUSTRATIONS
COLORING BOOK

SQUARE BOY
COLORING BOOK
FOR MINECRAFTERS

POW
Blank
Comic Book
Draw Your Own Comics
!!!
WOW

SONIC
SUPER MARIO
COLORING BOOK
JUMBO
2 IN 1

LEGO
STAR WARS
COLORING BOOK

SUPER
MARIO™
COLORING BOOK

SONIC
COLORING BOOK

Disney
THE LITTLE
MERMAID
COLORING BOOK

5 IN 1
NINJAGO
STAR WARS
LEGO
CHIMA
JUMBO COLORING BOOK
CITY
BIONICLE

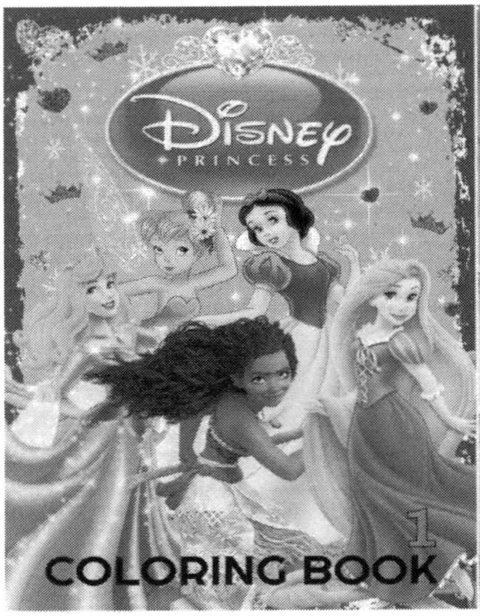
Disney
PRINCESS
1
COLORING BOOK

Disney
PRINCESS
2
COLORING BOOK

Disney's
BEAUTY AND THE BEAST
COLORING BOOK

Disney
FROZEN

Disney
PRINCESS
2
COLORING BOOK

Disney
THE LITTLE MERMAID
COLORING BOOK

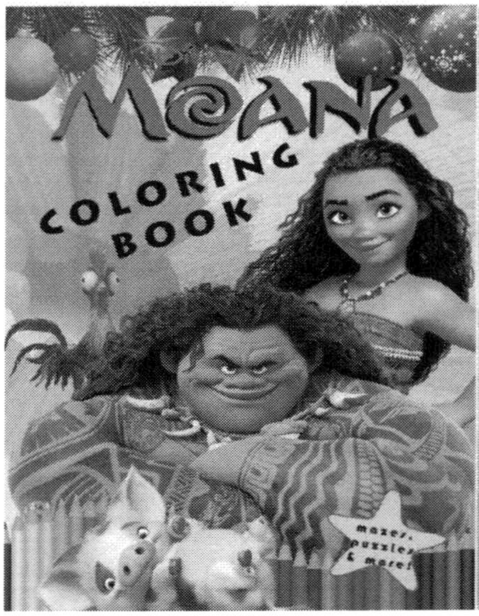
MOANA
COLORING
BOOK
mazes, puzzles & more!

Snow White
and the Seven Dwarfs
COLORING BOOK

Disney
Tangled
COLORING BOOK
Great Coloring Book For Fans of this Wonderful Cartoon

15319187R10097

Made in the USA
Middletown, DE
21 November 2018